HAVE-A-BLAST GAMES
FOR YOUTH GROUPS

Compiled by the Editors of Group Publishing

Group Books

Loveland, Colorado

Have-a-Blast Games for Youth Groups

Copyright © 1991 by Group Publishing, Inc.
Second Printing, 1992

Credits
Edited by Michael Warden and Stephen Parolini
Cover and Interior Designed by Jill Christopher
Illustrations by Jan Knudson

Library of Congress Cataloging-in-Publication Data
Have-a-blast games for youth groups / compiled by the editors
of Group Publishing.
     p.   cm.
     ISBN 1-55945-046-0 :
1. Group games.   I. Group Publishing.
GV1203.H399 1991
790.1—dc20   91-3288
                                     CIP

Printed in the United States of America

CONTENTS

Remarkable Recreations...........53

Dynamic Diversions

NTRODUCTION

Teenagers love to play games. But coming up with new and exciting games to use with your youth group is often time-consuming and tedious.

Not any more. Scan the contents of this book, and you'll find the perfect game for your group.

Have-a-Blast Games for Youth Groups is a compilation of over 100 creative ideas that'll involve your youth group in tons of fun. The simple directions and few or no materials needed, allow you to select an activity and start—all within a matter of minutes.

These ideas will energize group members and help break the ice at meetings, retreats, lock-ins or wherever you want to have a good time. You'll find:

● Crazy Competitions (team games);

● Remarkable Recreations (one-on-one, partner and all-group games); and

● Dynamic Diversions (zany activities and games).

So go ahead—flip through the pages until you find a game that's right for your group. Be creative! Adapt, modify and expand the activities for your group's enjoyment. Then create new ideas—and send them to us. Just write:

"Try This One"
GROUP Magazine
Box 481
Loveland, CO 80539

You'll receive a check for each idea we publish.

CRAZY
COMPETITIONS

A PEELIN' BANANAS

This game is certainly appealing!

Form relay teams, and have them each line up at one end of the room. Set a chair for each team at the opposite end of the room.

CHOMP! CHOMP!

Give kids each a banana. Give a book to the first person on each team.

On "go," the first person on each team places the book on his or her head, walks to the chair, sits down and peels and eats the banana. Then the team member stands (with the book still on his or her head), returns to the starting line and hands the book to the next person in line. If a team member drops the book, he or she must start over.

Continue the relay until the last person on a team crosses the finish line and yells intelligibly, "A-peelin' bananas!"

BALLOON-BAG VOLLEYBALL

Here's a volleyball variation you can do with a trash bag and a few balloons.

Set up a volleyball net and form teams. Instead of a volleyball, use a large plastic bag (33-gallon size or larger) filled with inflated balloons and sealed at the opening with duct tape. Basic volleyball rules apply except that kids may hit the "ball" up to six times per side, and they may *not* use their hands or arms. Because the ball is so light, kids will be able to keep it in the air with their heads and feet.

BASKET-BASEBALL

It's two ... two ... two sports in one!

Form two teams. Give team 1 newspaper batons or bats and give team 2 a large supply of newspaper wads. Put a washtub on the floor. Measure a 6-foot radius from the tub's edge, and make a circle around the tub with masking tape.

Have members of team 1 lie on their backs with their heads toward the tub and their feet toward the tape. Have members of team 2 sit cross-legged around the outside of the tape. When you blow the whistle, kids on team 2 should try to throw the newspaper wads into the tub while kids on team 1 guard the tub with their newspaper bats. After 30 seconds, blow the whistle and count the wads in the tub. Then switch teams.

For extra fun, try more teams and have a tournament!

BEACH VOLLEYBALL

Here's a great old favorite with a twist!

Set up a volleyball net in an open area, and mark boundaries. Form two teams, and have team members pair up. Give each pair a beach towel. Play volleyball using a beach ball. Kids may not touch the ball with their bodies; they must play by hitting the ball with a beach towel stretched between partners. The ball may be passed to other team pairs any number of times before it goes over the net. But if the ball touches the ground, the opposing team scores or wins possession of the serve.

BIBLICAL SPIN-A-FORTUNE

This game makes learning fun. Watch kids enjoy learning biblical facts as they spin the arrow.

Make a game board using a 2- to 3-foot-square piece of $^3/_4$-inch plywood. On the wood, sketch a circle and divide it into 12 even pie shapes. Paint each pie shape a different bright color. Label the pie shapes. Make two each of 50, 100, 200 and 300. Make one each of 500, "free spin," "bankrupt," and "lose spin." Use a nail to attach a large cardboard arrow spinner to the middle of the circle.

Write or choose from a Bible quiz book questions that have definite one- to five-word answers. Use newsprint or a blackboard to create a word puzzle for each answer. For example, draw 15 blank squares (like you do in the game Hangman) for an answer such as "twelve disciples."

Form teams. Read aloud a question. Have kids from each team take turns spinning the arrow and guessing the missing letters of each word puzzle. For example, if the arrow points to 100, a team member earns 100 points for guessing a missing letter in the mystery word or phrase. If that person guesses an "e" for the puzzle "twelve disciples," his or her team gets 300 points (three "e's"). If a team member guesses a letter not in the word or phrase, the next team gets to spin. As long as a team member guesses correctly, he or she keeps spinning.

If a team member spins the arrow to "bankrupt," his or her team loses all its points. If the arrow points to "lose spin," the team misses its turn. But if the arrow points to "free spin," the team gets to spin twice. As team members guess the letters, fill in the squares on the transparency. The game ends when all the letters are filled in. The team with the most points wins.

BLOW BALL

Here's a crazy but simple game youth groups love. All you need is a table, a Ping-Pong ball and some crackers. Form two teams. Have each team kneel and form an L around two sides of the table. Their hands must be kept under the table, and their chins must remain resting on the table edge.

The object of the game is to blow the ball off the other team's side of the table. Each time the ball is blown off, the blowing team scores a point. The first team to score 7 points wins.

To start each round of the game, place a Ping-Pong ball in the middle of the table and "feed" each person a cracker. Have kids each start blowing the ball once they've finished their cracker. Stand back—far back—and watch the fun.

BOBSLED RELAY

Here's a way to enjoy "bobsled" races in the middle of summer!

You'll need a large carpeted floor for the racing area. Mark starting and finish lines at least 20 feet apart using masking tape. Tear wax paper into 4-foot lengths.

Form pairs. Give each pair a bobsled (wax-paper sheet). Have pairs join together to form equal teams of four to 10.

Have one pair from each team place its "bobsled" behind the starting line. Have the starting pairs each decide which partner will sit on the bobsled and which will stand behind the bobsled. On "go," have the standing partners each push their teammate to the finish line, switch places with their partner, then return to the starting line on their bobsled. As soon as a pair returns to its starting line, the next pair can begin to race.

The first team to have all its pairs complete the course wins the game.

BOTTOM BALL

If your group needs a crazy indoor game, this one is for you.

Form four teams. Make a "net" by suspending crepe paper from four tall objects, such as teenagers, pillars or stacks of chairs. The net should be 4 feet off the floor and in the form of an X. You'll need several beach balls or balloons.

Have each team sit on the floor in one of the "courts." Say: **The object of the game is to keep the balloons or balls from touching the floor in your court. Hit the balls over the net just as you would for volleyball, with one exception: Don't let your rear end leave the floor!**

To add more fun and chaos, try tossing in more balls.

Bottom Basketball

This idea utilizes the same concept as Bottom Ball. Place a wastebasket on a chair at each end of the playing room. Form two teams. Then follow all the rules of basketball with these exceptions:

Players must sit on their bottoms for the duration of the game.

Rather than dribbling the ball, players must bounce the ball after every three "scoots" they take on their bottoms.

BROOM RIDE

Make a clean sweep with this team game.

You'll need three brooms approximately the same size. Have three teams each line up behind a designated line with their broom. When you say "ride," each team must stay behind the line and put as many players as possible on its broomstick. Then players must "ride" the broom to a chosen end point. The riders must return to the starting line if anyone falls off the broom. If all the players don't fit on the broom, one person must run back on the broom to get the other players. The first team to get all its players across the finish line wins.

ELF DEFENSE

Form two teams of elves. Each team must defend its treasure (a pile of balloons) while attempting to steal or destroy the other team's treasure. Use one color of balloons for one team, and another color for the other team. Designate a time period (five to 10 minutes) to play the game. When the time ends, each team's unpopped balloons count 100 points each. Stolen, unpopped balloons count 200 points each.

FLASHLIGHT FLOOR HOCKEY

Add spice to a game already popular with young people. Acquire a floor hockey set (brooms and balls will also work) and two flashlights. Build your own goals, or at each end of the court lay a rectangular church table on its side with the feet against the wall and the table top facing the playing area.

Form two teams. Have one person from each team stand against the wall at half court on opposite sides. They must stay at this position throughout the game. Give these two people each a flashlight. Then turn off the lights! Let the two teams play floor hockey as the flashlights provide the only light source.

Outlaw physical contact among players by penalizing violators with a two-minute penalty (they're out of the game for two minutes). Give the same penalty to those who lift their sticks above the waist in windup or follow-through. Have a devotional afterward about teamwork, or discuss the value of rules and penalties in the Christian life.

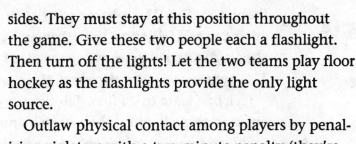

FRIENDSHIP RELAY

Here's a different kind of friendship race for your kids.

You'll need a stopwatch, a flashlight for each person, and bandannas. Set up boundaries for a figure-eight racecourse using soft objects such as pillows or sweat shirts. Form teams of three. Have each team designate one member as the Rider and the other two as the Carriers. The Carriers will get on all fours side by side. Tie their wrists and ankles together with bandannas. The Rider will sit on top of the Carriers as they race the figure-eight course.

Turn off the lights, and have kids turn on their

flashlights. Say: <u>**The object of this race is for each team's Rider to spur his or her Carriers through the racecourse from start to finish. The team with the shortest time wins.**</u>

Pick one team to go first. Tell the rest of the teams to shine light on the course by turning their flashlights on and off quickly, for a strobe-light effect. Time how long each team takes to run the course. Then give the members of the fastest team each a bandanna to remind them of their "ties" of friendship.

HULA-HOOP HYSTERIA

For some hilarious havoc, try Hula Hoop Hysteria!
Form teams of no more than five. Then have
teams compete in the following activities:

● Hula-Hands-Off Relay—Have teammates form a
straight line and hold hands. Place a Hula Hoop
over the head of the person at the front of the line.
Then have the team members get the Hula Hoop to
the end of the line and back to the beginning without letting go of each other's hands. Kids may not
grab the Hula Hoop; they must wiggle and climb
through it until it reaches the next person. The first
team to get the Hula Hoop back to the front of the
line wins.

● Hula-Wheels Relay—Set up a goal, such as a
chair, at one end of the room. Have teams line up at
the opposite end. One at a time, have teammates
roll the Hula Hoop like a wheel to the opposite end
of the room, around the goal and back again. Then
have them roll it to the next teammate. The first
team to complete the relay wins.

● Hula-Tube Relay—Have team members stand in
a circle with space between them. Have the first
person drop the Hula Hoop over his or her head. As
soon as it hits the floor, have that person step out
and the next person step in. Then have that person
pull the Hula Hoop up over his or her head. Then

have that team member step out while another person steps under the Hula Hoop. Proceed in this way until the Hula Hoop makes it around the circle. The first team to finish wins.

● Hula Hoop Obstacle Course—Set up a miniature obstacle course, either inside or outside. Then, one at a time, have team members run through the obstacle course while swinging the Hula Hoop around their hips. The first team to finish wins.

● Hula Hoop-Off—For the grand finale, gather as many Hula Hoops as possible. Then, using them in hula fashion, see which team can keep the most Hula Hoops going for the longest time.

Award Hawaiian prizes, such as leis, grass skirts or tapes of Elvis Presley's *Blue Hawaii* to the team that wins the most relays.

HUMAN CHECKERS

This game is sure to add life to your youth group meeting. And it's a way to get a lot of kids involved.

Tape alternating pieces of red and black construction paper in checkerboard-style in a large area. There should be eight rows of eight squares. Each square area should be large enough for a person to sit on. Make sure the lower left corner of the "board" is black.

Ask 24 kids to be "checkers"—12 black and 12 red. Have them each tape a square of red or black paper to their shoulder, according to their checker color. Tell them they can only move to black squares.

Choose two kids who understand the game to be the players. Have them stand on chairs to see the overall board. Have them move their "checkers," following the rules of checkers.

To jump, the jumping checker must leapfrog over

the other checker. When a player is eliminated, he or she must wait until needed to "crown" a teammate. Then he or she stands behind the checker that is crowned.

Continue until one team eliminates the other.

MINIATURE HOCKEY

Here's a game that'll bring your kids to their knees.

Form two teams of four, and give each team member a Popsicle stick. Designate a "goal-holder" for each team. Have the goal-holders each kneel at opposite ends of the room and hold a paper cup on the floor so the other team can drive a Ping-Pong ball into it successfully. Emphasize that the goal-holders shouldn't try to obstruct the ball.

Tell teams the object of the game is to get the ball into their team's "goal." The catch is: Players must each place their stick in their mouth and use it to move their ball. Kids may use their hands for support. Remind them to use caution.

On "go," drop the ball in the middle of the playing area, and watch teams go after it.

Have any extra people stand on the sidelines to cheer. Rotate players in after each goal so everyone gets to play.

To make the game more of a challenge, use two different-color Ping-Pong balls, and have four teams play at the same time.

MUSCLE BEACH

Use this activity to pump up your group!

Ask the guys in the group each to bring an oversize sweat shirt. Don't tell kids what the sweat shirts will be used for. Also, bring to the meeting 10 to 15 balloons for every four kids in your group. Keep the balloons in the packages until the activity begins.

Form teams of four with at least one guy on each team. Have each team choose a guy to represent it, then ask those chosen guys to come to the front and put on an oversize sweat shirt. Tell kids: **The object of this contest is to make a "muscle man" for "muscle beach." Each team will blow up, tie off and stuff as many balloons as it can into the sweat shirt of its muscle man. The goal is to make your guy as "muscular" as possible. You'll have just two minutes.**

Break open the packages of balloons, and put them in the center of the group. Blow a whistle to start the competition, and blow it again after two minutes. Have a panel of judges made up of sponsors or youth workers declare a winning muscle man. The first guy to break all his balloons by himself is also declared a winner. Reward the teams of both winners with Big Red gum or jawbreakers.

NAME THE TESTAMENT

Help kids learn the Bible while they have fun!

Form two teams. Hang two sheets of newsprint at one end of the room. On each, write "Old Testament," "Other," and "New Testament." Have each team line up at the opposite end of the room, one person behind the other, facing one of the newsprint sheets.

Tell kids you'll yell out a name—from the Bible or someplace else. Have the first teammates each run up to their team's newsprint and use their hands to frame the correct source. The team that correctly answers the questions first gets a point. Record teams' points on the newsprint. The team with the most points at the end wins.

OREO SCULPTURES

Form equal-size teams, and give each team several packages of Oreo cookies (or have kids bring their own). Also, give each team two serrated knives, two spoons, a box of toothpicks and a sheet of newsprint.

Say: <u>**Your team has 20 minutes to create a sculpture using the cookies and the tools**</u>

I've given you. Build your sculpture on the newsprint to help control the mess.

The white stuff in the Oreos makes great glue or mortar. The brittle part of the cookies can be cut, crushed or left whole to form creations such as a castle, a Mickey Mouse head or even a rolling Model T.

Have everyone vote on the most creative sculpture. Give the winning team a gallon of milk.

PET TALK

Will the real pet-owner please stand up? If you'd like your kids to learn more about one another, let their pets do the talking!

Have kids each write on a sheet of paper the names of their pets. Then form teams of three or more. Call the teams—one by one—to stand in front of the others. Read from that team's papers the names of three pets and have the other kids guess which pet names belong to which team members. Repeat the process until all teams have finished. Award fun pet prizes such as dog biscuits to the teammates whose pet names were easiest to match with their owners.

Your group is sure to discover hilarious pet names and learn new secrets about one another.

PHARAOH'S FOLLY

This wild relay plays upon the story of the plagues in Exodus 7-11.

Form teams of four. At one end of the room, blindfold three members of each team (to illustrate the plague of darkness). The fourth member of each team stands at the other end of the room. Place some marshmallows and a cup of red Kool-

Aid near him or her. Take precautions to protect the floor if necessary.

On "go," the blindfolded players begin leap-frogging (plague of frogs) toward their teammate, who may only "moo" like a cow (plague on live-stock) to give directions. Teams might want to work out a code beforehand, such as two "moos" mean "turn left."

Once leapfroggers reach their teammate, one blindfolded player must find the marshmallows (plague of hail) and red Kool-Aid (plague of blood). He or she then feeds the marshmallows to the second player and gives the Kool-Aid to the third player. Then the three blindfolded teammates turn around and leapfrog back to where they began after the fourth teammate runs to the other end and guides them with more "moos." The team that finishes first wins.

PROGRESSIVE RELAY

Use this relay to teach your kids the value of teamwork.

Set two chairs at one end of the meeting room. On each chair, place a stack of 3×5 cards on which you've written relay instructions kids will carry out

(see the samples below). You'll need one-half as many instructions as you have kids, and a set of them for each team. Shuffle each set of instructions independently.

Form two teams. Have teams line up in single-file lines on the side of the room opposite the chairs. On "go," the first person on each team will run to the chair, take one 3×5 card, follow the instructions, tag the chair, run back to his or her team and lock arms with the next person in line. Both of them will run back to the chair, take one 3×5 card, follow the instructions together, tag the chair, lock arms again, run back to their team and lock arms with the third person, and so on. This continues until all team members have been included, finished the instructions and run back to their starting line. Award prizes to the team that finishes first.

Sample Relay Instructions

- Sing "Jingle Bells."
- Do five jumping jacks.
- Run around the room.
- Take off your shoes.
- Run backward to your team.
- Get a drink of water.
- Hop to your team.
- Run around the chair two times yelling your school's name.
- Kneel and say, "Jesus rules!"

SAILING RELAY

Do your kids like to sail? Then indulge them in this sailing relay!

Place a half-filled wading pool at one end of a large, open area. Form three or more teams. Have each team line up, single file, at the other end of the open area. Give each team a beach towel and a

plastic foam cup. The pool should have a large X marked on the inside wall farthest from the kids.

Say: **When I blow the whistle, the first person on each team should run to the pool, place the towel on the ground, kneel on the towel, place the cup in the water and blow it toward the X on the opposite side of the pool. When the cup touches the X, pick up your towel, grab your cup and race back to your team. Give the towel and the cup to the next team member and continue the relay. If your cup sinks, you must start again from the front of the pool.**

The first team to have all its members "navigate" successfully, wins.

SNAKE RACE

Here's a fun way to race as a team!

Ask kids to wear old clothing. Form two teams. Have kids on each team lie face down—head to toe—and grab one another's ankles. Then have the two teams race down a hallway to a finish line by squirming along the floor like snakes.

SNOWSHOE RELAY

Want winter in July? Here's one way to do it!
Borrow, buy or rent two pairs of snowshoes. Have
kids create a "mountain" out of crumpled newspapers. Then form two teams, and have kids wearing
snowshoes run a relay race over your "mountain."

SQUIRT-GUN VOLLEYBALL

Ask kids to each bring a squirt gun to the meeting. Outline with a string a rectangular playing area
somewhere outside. Divide the playing area in half
with a tape line on the ground. Form two teams,
and have them each sit inside the playing area on
either side of the divider line (the net).

Inflate a balloon. Play volleyball using the balloon as the ball. Tell kids they must use their squirt
guns, not their hands or feet, to push the ball over
the net. Unlike regular volleyball, they're allowed to
use an unlimited number of squirts to push the

balloon over the line. If the balloon touches the ground on team 1's side, it's team 2's point (and vice versa).

STEAL-IT

Here's a fun game for a rainy day.

Form two teams. Give one team a bunch of red objects. Give the other team the same number of blue objects. Objects could be items such as socks, balls, toys, candy, pencils and crayons. Have the teams hide the objects around the meeting area. Then on "go," let each team's members "steal" as many of the objects hidden by the other team as they can find. Kids cannot defend the locations of their team's objects. After a few minutes, stop the game. Count the number of items stolen by each team and declare a winner.

STRESS POINTS

Use masking tape to make two parallel lines on the floor, about 2 feet apart. The area between the lines will be the "neutral zone." Make the lines long enough for half your group to stand comfortably along each line.

Form two teams. Have teams each stand behind their line, facing the other team. Tell teams they're going to play a variation of Tug of War. Teams will each "invite" the opposing team members to join their team by dragging them into the neutral zone. When a team gets an opposing team member into the neutral zone, that person becomes a supportive member of the new team and helps pull other people into the zone. Teams can try anything to resist having team members pulled into the neutral zone, but when a person's foot enters the neutral zone, that person has to join the other team. Have teams stay close to their lines.

Encourage teams to let their team members know how cherished and valuable they are by grabbing on to them and saving them from being pulled away. Caution kids not to hurt each other.

Let the game continue until everyone is on the same team. Then talk about the importance of overlooking prejudices and joining together as one team.

TEETH FREEZE

Break the ice—literally—with this crowdbreaker.
Give each group member a Popsicle. Form teams.
Have the first person on each team eat his or her
Popsicle, then the second person, and so on. The
first team to have all its members finish their
Popsicles wins. Take lots of photographs!

TEN-NERFING

Here's a game that's certain to cool off a hot day! It combines softball, tennis, Nerf balls and water into a wet and wonderful team sport.

You'll need two large Nerf balls, a large bucket of water and a tennis racket. Ask kids to dress in T-shirts and shorts, or swimsuits.

Form two teams. Explain that the game is played much like softball. The tennis racket substitutes for the bat and the Nerf balls replace the softball. The Nerf balls are soaked in water before they're pitched. One soaks in the bucket of water while the other is being pitched.

Each batter has only three tries to hit the wet Nerf ball. An out occurs when the batter fails to hit one of the three pitches or when a runner is hit by the wet Nerf ball while trying to reach a base. Each team is allowed three outs each time at bat.

Play as many innings as you like!

3-PASS BASKETBALL

For a hoppin' good time, try this basketball game.

Gather one medium-size foam basketball and two small, kid-size basketball hoops. Mount the hoops on chairs.

Form teams. Have everyone sit cross-legged. Start the game with a jump ball. Have team members pass the ball a minimum of three times before they shoot.

Each time players get the ball, they must hop or scoot in cross-legged position two times before getting rid of the ball. Each basket is 1 point. The first team to score 10 points wins.

Other basketball rules are optional. The fewer rules, the more fun.

TRIANGLE VOLLEYBALL

Here's a newfangled volleyball game that really works. Form three teams—A, B and C. Set up a triangle of chairs, 10 chairs to a side. Each wall of chairs serves as a "net." Place tape onto the floor to extend the boundaries of the triangle. Have each team sit on the floor in a line behind its net, facing inward. Players must stay seated. Play begins when a referee bounces a volleyball or beach ball in the middle of the triangle.

Teams A, B and C play against one another at the same time. Refer to the diagram for how to allocate points. When the ball hits the floor in a particular zone, the point goes to the team(s) circled.

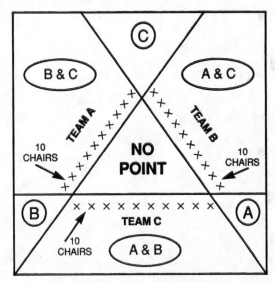

TRIPLE SOFTBALL

Everyone knows how to play softball with two teams, but why not try playing with three teams? Make sure teams each have an equal number of players—at least five. All the normal rules of softball apply.

The game starts with team 1 at bat and teams 2 and 3 out in the field. After team 1 has three outs, team 2 is at bat and teams 1 and 3 play the field. After team 2 has three outs, team 3 is at bat and teams 1 and 2 play the field, and so on. After each team has been at bat three times, tally each one's score and declare the winner.

TURTLE RELAY

This activity will help kids come out of their shells!

Find two dishwasher or washing-machine packing boxes to use as turtle shells. Halfway up one side of each box, cut a hole that's big enough for a teenager to stick his or her head through. Then cut out the bottom of each box.

Form two relay teams. The object is for kids to run the relay race like turtles—crawling to a specified point while underneath the box, then returning to tag the next teammate. The first team to have all its "turtles" complete the course wins.

WACKYBALL

Looking for a wacky outdoor game that's sure to be a hit with your group? Look no further! This game gets its wacky name because there's no telling how the ball will bounce when it's hit.

You'll need a Nerf football, a softball bat and bases. Lay out the bases in a square approximately 30 feet apart.

Form two teams. For each team, you'll need a pitcher, a catcher, a shortstop, basemen and outfielders.

Play the game much like softball, pitching the Nerf football underhand. Allow only two outs per team to keep the game moving.

Happy wackyball!

WIN-OR-LOSE OBSTACLE COURSE

Let kids have fun with this zany race idea!
Form two teams. Have them run two short,
identical obstacle courses like a relay. For example, a
course might have:

● three chairs tied together—kids wriggle
through the legs

● lines of tape a yard apart—kids do standing
long jumps from one mark to the other

● a podium—kids run around this three times

● a kindergarten-size chair—kids sit down in it
and walk forward four steps, then backward four
steps

After both teams finish, announce the winner.

YUMMY

Break the ice with this tasty game. Kids eat it up! Form teams of six. Give each team a cup of plain M&M's and a paper plate. Have the first person on each team dump the cup of M&M's onto the paper plate and eat only the yellow ones. When finished, he or she puts the remaining M&M's back into the cup and passes it on. The second person repeats the same process and eats only the orange M&M's. Remaining team members continue to take turns eating the other colors. Give a five-second penalty for every M&M dropped on the floor.

The team that finishes its M&M's first is the winner.

REMARKABLE RECREATIONS

BLOB TAG

You saw the movie, now, here's the game! You'll have a "mass" of fun with this one!

Choose one person to be "It." "It" calls out any number, then shouts out the letters B-L-O-B! While "It" is yelling letters, everyone else forms "blobs" of whatever number was called out. After "It" finishes yelling B-L-O-B, he or she should try to tag someone who's not already in a blob. The first person tagged becomes the new "It."

BODY SCRATCH

Use this activity as a crowdbreaker. Before everyone arrives, write the following words in big letters on a sheet of newsprint:

Head	Back
Knee	Stomach
Elbow	Shoulder
Foot	Nose

Show kids the newsprint list. Say: **I'm going to blow a whistle and point to one of the words on this list. The word I point to is the body part you'll need to scratch for someone else in the room. I'll also call out a number. The number represents the number of people you'll have to scratch.**

For example, when you blow the whistle, point to the the word "Back" and call out "six," kids should run around and scratch six other people's backs. Then blow the whistle and repeat the procedure with another body part and number. You may repeat body parts but not in succession. Keep the activity moving by blowing the whistle quickly (before everyone finishes the previous action).

This activity will help kids relieve tension and have a good time.

CALENDAR SEARCH

Bring old calendars, and give one to each person. Form teams, and give each team a few calendars. Call out holidays from the following list one at a time. The first person or team to find the holiday on the calendar wins that round. The holidays:

- Mother-in-Law Day
- Hanukkah
- Palm Sunday
- Canada Day
- Father's Day
- Martin Luther King Jr. Day
- Passover
- Election Day
- Rosh Hashana
- Flag Day
- Easter
- Veterans Day
- Victoria Day
- Grandparents Day
- Yom Kippur
- Presidents' Day
- Thanksgiving Day (Canada)
- Memorial Day
- St. Patrick's Day
- Columbus Day
- Mother's Day
- Labor Day

CAN STACKS

Form teams of three. Have teams each find a separate area in the room. Have teams each use masking tape to "draw" a circular boundary (about 5 feet in diameter) around their team.

Give teams each the same number of empty soft-drink cans (at least 15) and marshmallows. On "go," have teams compete to see who can stack all the cans in a single tower. Only one can may serve as the base. Tell teams they may attempt to topple other teams' towers by tossing marshmallows toward them.

Kids may not leave their circular boundaries or hold their towers of cans. If towers are toppled, kids must begin stacking cans again. Watch to see which team stacks all the cans first. Award that team a package of marshmallows as a prize.

ELBOW TAG

Here's an old game with a new "bent."

Say: **Form a circle of pairs, leaving one pair outside the circle. Kids in the circle should keep arms linked with their partners but not with other pairs in the circle. The "left-out" pair should unlink arms and decide who will be the "Chaser" and who will be the "Chased." Chaser chases Chased around and through the circle of pairs. Chased may run around and through the circle but not out of the immediate area of the group. If Chaser tags Chased, they change roles. Tag-backs are allowed. Chased can avoid being tagged by linking elbows with the free arm of a member of one of the pairs. The other member of that pair then becomes "Chased" and must run and/or link arms with someone else.**

Play until everyone has had a chance to be the Chaser or until time runs out.

FAMOUS ANIMAL CROWDBREAKER

Write the names of famous cartoon animals on separate sheets of paper. Names could include Road Runner, Bugs Bunny, Tweety, Scooby Doo, Daffy Duck and Roger Rabbit. Attach one name to the back of each young person without letting the person know what name you're attaching. Then have kids each ask each other yes-or-no questions about the cartoon animal that's named on their back until they guess correctly.

FLASHLIGHT-FINDERS

This bright game works best at night or in a darkened building.

Form pairs. Have one pair hide 10 turned-on flashlights around the church. Flashlights may not be completely covered. Have the other pairs hold hands and race to see how many flashlights they can find within five minutes. For each flashlight that's found, award 5 points to the pair that found it. For each flashlight that's not found, award 5 points to the pair that hid it.

Be sure pairs each get at least one opportunity to hide the flashlights. Keep a running score and award a prize, such as a package of batteries, to the pair with the most points.

FROZEN-BUBBLE FOLLIES

Are you at a loss for a fun, outdoor, wintertime activity? Here's one that's guaranteed to blow your group away!

On cold, clear, moonlit January nights in northern areas, old-fashioned bubble-blowing is a whole new experience—the bubbles freeze! And if the moon isn't cooperating, an outdoor spotlight is nearly as effective at adding extra dazzle to the frozen bubbles.

At least four hours before the meeting, prepare plenty of bubble solution using six cups water, 2 cups liquid dish soap, ¾ cup clear corn syrup and food coloring.

When kids arrive, form teams of no more than five. Have kids raid the kitchen for creative bubble-blowing paraphernalia, such as spatulas, strainers or string. Then go outside and have each team present its bubble-blowing extravaganza for the other teams.

Award bubble gum to teams that create the biggest bubble, the smallest bubble and the longest-lasting bubble, and that use the most interesting bubble-blowing paraphernalia.

THE GREAT GUMSHOE

Have kids mix up their shoes in a pile at one end of the room. Form teams of four or more at the opposite end of the room.

The first person on each team is the "detective." The second person on each team describes his or her shoes to the detective, who runs to find them in the shoe pile and bring them back.

If the detective brings back the wrong shoes, he or she gathers more clues and searches again. If the detective brings back the right shoes, the owner puts them on and becomes the detective. Repeat the process until one team finds all its shoes.

GROUP TRIVIAL PURSUIT

Kick off an activity with this mind-boggling crowdbreaker.

Set your memory and creativity in motion by creating "Trivial Pursuit" cards—each with a question based on a bizarre or outrageous group experience. For example:

● Which two guys were severely beaten in the Grand Slam Pillow Fight of 1991?

● Which girl is a certified scuba diver?

● Name five new seventh-graders in our group and introduce yourself to them.

Give group members each a different Group Trivial Pursuit question card and a pencil. Kids can find answers by mixing with and asking other group members questions. Award a prize to the person who's first to finish.

JELLYBEAN JAM

Here's an idea for getting an unfamiliar group to interact. For each person, insert nine different-color jellybeans in an envelope.

Give an envelope of jellybeans to each person. Say: **The object of this game is to get nine jellybeans of the same color. You have to ask others for the color of jellybean you want and then trade one of yours. You may trade only one jellybean at a time.**

This activity takes time because several people may be pursuing jellybeans of the same color. The first person to get nine same-color jellybeans is the winner.

If you have fewer than nine people in your group, place fewer jellybeans in each envelope, and have kids try to get that number of same-color jellybeans. If you have more than nine people in your group, be sure to have at least nine jellybeans of each color spread among the envelopes.

JUNK MIXER

Do you have a problem with cliques within your group? Or are there new kids in your group? If so, use this crowdbreaker to get group members talking with each other.

Collect ordinary, small household items, such as a button, eraser, rubber band, Popsicle stick, thimble, pencil or emery board. You'll need one item for each group member. List the items on a sheet of paper with a line beside each item. Make one photocopy of the list for each participant.

Put each item in an envelope. As kids arrive, hand them each an envelope and a photocopied list. Explain that each group member must somehow wear his or her item. Have kids each find out who's wearing each item and write that person's name in the appropriate place on the list.

MASTERPIECE-IN-A-MINUTE

Are your teenagers always competing to see "who's the best"? Or are you looking for ways to put their creativity "to the test"? In either case, the following activity is sure to register a winner!

You'll need finger paints, aprons, paper and a prize of some kind.

Give each group member three different colors of finger paint, an apron and a sheet of paper. Then have "artists" each create a "masterpiece" in one minute's time using only their nose to apply the paint. For a variation, blindfold the artists.

Have the group vote on the best painting, and award a prize to the winner.

 NAME SHUFFLE

This activity will help kids get to know each other better.

Give kids each a 3×5 card. Instruct kids to each write their first name on their card. Have them place all the cards in a basket. Then shuffle the cards and tape one to each teenager's back without letting the teenager read the name on it. Make sure no one gets his or her own name.

Then challenge your kids to each discover whose name is on their back by asking other kids questions that can only be answered yes or no. (They can't ask, "Is it [name]?")

When kids each discover the name on their back, they should find that person and ask: "What's one thing you like to do? one place you like to go?"

After getting answers to the questions, have kids help each other discover the name on their back. When all are finished have kids each tell the group what they discovered.

NAME THAT PERSON!

Would you expect to find "Clay" working in a pottery shop? Or how about "Rose" tending a garden?

Give each kid a "Names!" handout [page 70]. Then have individuals or teams compete to see who can come up with the most names. After 10 minutes, call time. Use the "Answers" box below to see how kids did.

Answers
Name That Girl—(1) Melody; (2) Dawn; (3) Pearl; (4) April, May or June; (5) Lily or Daisy; (10) Constance; (11) Fanny; (12) Joy, Gladys, Mary or Merry; (13) Candy; (6) Sandy; (7) Pat, Margie or Marjorene; (8) Lisa or Aleese; (9) Rose, Violet, Charity or Sharon.

Name That Guy—(1) Stu; (2) Jack; (3) Woody, Buzz or Chip; (4) Nicholas; (5) Clay; (6) Bill; (7) Scott; (8) Chuck; (9) Marlin; (10) Barry; (11) Frank; (12) Cliff; (13) Curt an' Rod.

Names!

Instructions: Some names just seem to fit who people are or what they do. How many names can you think of that match these descriptions? Write them on the lines following the clues.

Name That Girl . . .

1. who sings well _____
2. who gets up early _____
3. who lives in an oyster _____
4. who lives on a calendar _____
5. who's sweet _____
6. who lives on the beach _____
7. who lives in a butter dish _____
8. who rents out apartments _____
9. who lives in a flower garden _____
10. who's always consistent _____
11. who cools everyone off _____
12. who's a very happy person _____
13. who gives away her possessions _____

Name That Guy . . .

1. who's in a pot with carrots and potatoes _____
2. who lifts a car _____
3. who lives in a sawmill _____
4. who gave all his change away _____
5. who makes pottery _____
6. who's always in the mailbox _____
7. who lives in a paper-towel dispenser _____
8. who's tossed into a meat grinder _____
9. who swims in the ocean _____
10. who grows on bushes _____
11. who always says what he thinks _____
12. who lives on the edge _____
13. (twins) who are always near a window _____

NEIGHBORLY CHAIRS

Here's a fun variation of Musical Chairs. Make a circle of chairs, facing inward. Have one less chair than people.

Have your group members sit down. The person without a chair must stand in the center of the circle.

Have the person in the middle ask someone, "Do you love your neighbor?" If the person answers no, then that person and the person on either side of him or her try to switch chairs. The person in the middle tries to get an empty chair. No one may return to his or her original chair. One person will always be left standing in the center of the circle.

If the person answers yes, then that person must add "but I don't like anyone who's wearing red" (or some other description). All people who fit the description must find a new seat.

After the game, you may want to lead a Bible study on love using Luke 10:25-37; 1 Corinthians 13; and 1 John 4:7-8.

NOVEL QUEST

Here's an easy game with lots of variations kids will go crazy over.

Meet in a large room. Form teams of four to six, and have each team find a separate place to stand in the room. Use masking tape to place one X on the floor in the front of the room for every two teams. For example, if you have four teams, place two X's. If you have an odd number of teams, round up to the next even number. For example, if you have five teams, place three X's. Evenly space the X's along the floor so kids won't trip over one another when they run up to stand on an X. Prepare point tokens, such as slips of paper, beans or play money.

Say: **This contest is a variation of a scavenger hunt. I'll call out things for you to find. When you find the item I've called out,**

you must send a representative from your team with the item to one of the X's on the floor. If you get to one of the X's first, and you have the item, you'll get a token. At the end of the game, the team with the most tokens wins.

But be warned! You may not run or push people off an X. If all the X's are full, don't leave—someone might not have the correct item.

Some of the items on each list are written as riddles. Don't read aloud what's in the parentheses—that's what you're looking for. Let kids creatively figure out the puzzling scavenger-hunt items.

Choose a list of items to call out from any of the themes listed here. Mix and match items from different lists, or make up your own. This is a game that can be played over and over without repeating the same theme twice.

Theme: **Fashion**

- a ring you don't wear on your finger (earring)
- lace (shoelace or lace)
- a tool used in a manicure
- ring around the collar (necklace)
- a girl with a fake beard
- set of black teeth (comb)
- someone with a sock in his or her mouth
- a perfectly round hole in leather (hole in a belt or purse strap)
- someone wearing a T-shirt as a pair of pants
- a guy wearing fingernail polish

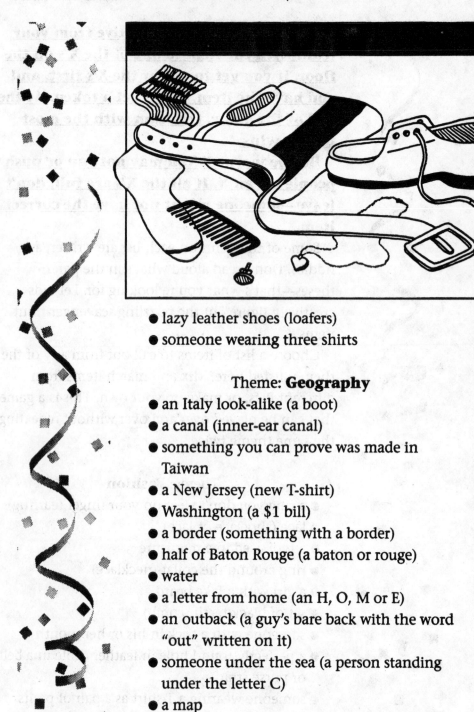

- lazy leather shoes (loafers)
- someone wearing three shirts

Theme: **Geography**
- an Italy look-alike (a boot)
- a canal (inner-ear canal)
- something you can prove was made in Taiwan
- a New Jersey (new T-shirt)
- Washington (a $1 bill)
- a border (something with a border)
- half of Baton Rouge (a baton or rouge)
- water
- a letter from home (an H, O, M or E)
- an outback (a guy's bare back with the word "out" written on it)
- someone under the sea (a person standing under the letter C)
- a map

Theme: **Hollywood**

- a camera
- two black eyes (a pair of sunglasses)
- a star (any star shape or a picture of a movie star)
- Jaws 3 (three sets of jaws)
- a frame (picture or glasses frame)
- a ticket or ticket stub
- an autograph
- E.T. (the letters E and T)
- script for the epic motion picture *The Ten Commandments* (a Bible)
- spotlight (flashlight)
- megaphone
- a topless guy wearing a Batman cape made from three T-shirts tied together

Theme: **Jesus' Life**

- a pair of sandals
- parables (pair of bowls)
- a palm leaf (a leaf drawn on someone's palm)
- two things that are healed (two feet, socks or shoes)
- Jesus' biography (the gospels—Bible must be opened to one of the right books)
- two people singing "Jesus Loves Me"
- someone walking on water (a person standing on spilled water)
- anointing oils (perfume)
- broken bread (piece of bread)
- talents—according to Jesus' parable of the talents (money)

- a cross
- someone pointing to the "lamp of the body" (an eye)

Theme: **Romantic Love**

- two pairs of matching socks
- kiss paint (lipstick)
- a love note
- a date (such as January 5)
- a broken heart (a torn heart shape)
- a guy gargling
- a finger loop (a ring)
- a guy and a girl holding hands
- a girl carrying a guy over the threshold
- a flower (a picture or the real thing)
- deodorant
- a guy and a girl carrying a knot

Theme: **Money**

- a completely empty wallet
- exactly 67 cents
- a bundle of pointed sticks (on the back of a $1 bill)
- Monti's cello (the Monticello on the back of a nickel)
- something silver
- a Federal Reserve note (any currency with "FEDERAL RESERVE NOTE" printed on it)
- a check (√)
- a counterfeit $5 bill (drawn)
- someone dressed as a hobo
- a computer (a calculator)

- a person carrying an eye (on the back of a $1 bill)
- a gold bar (any gold-color bar)

Theme: **Music**

- a musical note (either sung or written on paper)
- a staff (musical staff or a long stick)
- a cassette or CD
- a band (a wristband)
- a digital wave (someone waving his or her fingers)
- a chorus line (someone singing a line of a chorus)
- something that goes with "roll" (a rock)
- string (regular string or a guitar string)
- a wrap (a coat)
- pianos have lots of these ... bring two (keys)
- a cymbal (anything that symbolizes something)
- a mouthpiece (a retainer)

Theme: **Old Testament**

- something made of wool
- a staff (a musical staff or a long walking stick)
- Lot's wife (salt)
- something that could be an idol (anything that can be worshiped, such as money)
- a red sea (a C written in red ink or cut out of red paper)
- the Ten Commandments (in Deuteronomy 5)
- someone dressed to look like a sheep
- a pyramid (made of people, or on the back of a $1 bill)

- coat of many colors
- what God formed us out of (dust or dirt)
- Joshua 1:8 (a Bible opened to Joshua 1:8)
- the name of King David's third-born son (Absalom)

Theme: **Prophets**

- a beard (on a coin)
- something fake and something real (for true and false prophets)
- watchman (a guy with a watch)
- the names of three minor prophets in the Old Testament
- a visionary spectacle (glasses)
- honey (boyfriend or girlfriend)
- a sign
- someone dressed as an angel
- the Word of the Lord (the Bible)
- a staff (a musical staff or a long walking stick)
- a biblical passage that describes a naked prophet (Isaiah 20:2; Micah 1:8)
- a guy wearing rags, yelling, "The end of the world! The end of the world!"

Theme: **School**

- a lock (of hair)
- a spiral (notebook)
- a fully visible spine (book spine)
- the last word (in any book)
- three people doing a school cheer
- footnote (a note written on a foot)
- a science experiment (testing gravity, flying a paper airplane)
- at least 300 days (calendar)

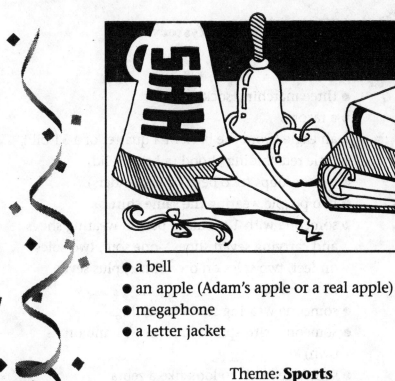

- a bell
- an apple (Adam's apple or a real apple)
- megaphone
- a letter jacket

Theme: **Sports**

- a quarterback (the real thing or the back of a quarter)
- a yard (three feet)
- a hoop (an earring)
- football (the real thing or the ball of someone's foot)
- a target drawn on someone's forehead
- a diamond
- a hole in one (a hole punched in the number "1")
- someone made to look like Arnold Schwarzenegger
- the end zone (someone's backside)
- a sweater
- a pitcher (of water)
- deodorant

Theme: **Mystery List**

- exactly $1.37
- 66 books
- three matching socks
- a razor
- an eagle (from the back of a quarter or a $1 bill)
- little red "hiding" hood (a lipstick lid)
- two holdups (two belts or suspenders)
- two people wearing the same shirt
- someone with 12 souls (a person wearing shoes and carrying seven shoes—one soul, two soles on feet, two soles on own shoes, plus seven more soles)
- someone wearing shoes as earrings
- someone with spiked hair (must stand on its own)
- someone made to look like a zebra

ORANGE BOWL

Announce that although one version of the Orange Bowl is played in Miami on New Year's Day, you're going to have your own version of this annual classic. Then bring out empty milk cartons and set them up at one end of the room as bowling pins. Have kids use an orange as a bowling ball, and see who can get the best score.

PAIR-O'-DICE

Here's a fun game to help your youth group members feel more comfortable sharing their feelings with each other.

Collect 4×4×4 white gift boxes from a local gift or jewelry store. Use the boxes to make a pair of "dice" for every six to eight kids in your group. On one side of each box draw a large, red triangle. Write one question on each of the remaining sides of the box. Questions can be related to your meeting's theme. Or they can be general questions; for example: What's one thing you like about yourself? What good thing happened to you in school this week? What's one thing you like about your best

friend? What's something you like about your family? What's one special thing about the person on your right?

To begin the game, form teams of six to eight, and have each team sit at a table. Give each team a pair of dice. The first player rolls the dice and answers either one of the questions that appear on the top of the dice. If one red triangle appears, all the kids must move to a new chair. If two red triangles appear, everyone must circle the table once and pass the chair they were in before finding a new seat. The dice always move to the next chair, so it's possible to avoid rolling the dice or it's possible to be always in control of the dice. Once kids notice that happening, there will be a mad rush for the same chair.

POETRY HODGEPODGE

Do you have a Shakespeare in your group? Here's a quick way to find out.

Form teams. Give each team an envelope containing a non-rhyming poem that's been cut into two-line pieces. Each envelope should have the same poem in it.

Ask teams each to reconstruct their poem as they think the author wrote it. Then have a person from each team read the revamped poem. The more variations, the better. After each team has shared its creative labor, read the true version of the poem.

This crowdbreaker also works at holiday parties when you use poems that reflect the occasion.

POSTCARD PASTE-UP

Use this fun crowdbreaker before a meeting about God's creation.

Collect about 40 picture postcards of scenery. Cut each in half. Place a card table with one-half of each postcard, a stapler and a few pencils in the center of the room. Place an empty wastebasket beside the table.

Hide the other halves of the postcards all over the room and anywhere else you want your kids to go.

On "go," have kids race to find the hidden postcard halves. When a group member finds a hidden half, he or she must run back to the table, staple it to the other half, sign it and "mail" it in the wastebasket.

When all the cards are mailed, count the signatures to discover who found the most. Give that person a prize of postage stamps.

REVERSE TAG

Get the group together in a large open space where kids can run. Select someone to be "It." Tell kids they're going to play an unusual game of Freeze Tag. When they're tagged, they must stand still until tagged by someone other than "It."

But Reverse Tag is slightly backward. Talk about how sacrifice is part of love and in this game kids will have the opportunity to "sacrifice" for others. Kids must try to "save" others from getting tagged by deliberately jumping in front of them to be tagged instead.

Tell kids they can't just run up and touch "It" to be tagged; they must actually be tagged.

Kids may need to think about this game for a few seconds before they catch on. Play Reverse Tag more than once for kids to play well.

SHOESTRING HOP

Here's a fun game to make refreshment time interesting.

Form a circle. Place at least one doughnut for each participant at various places around the room—out of kids' reach. Give two shoelaces to kids who aren't wearing shoes with laces.

On "go," have kids each connect their shoes with the shoes or ankles of the people on either side of them—using their shoe-laces. Then have the tied-together group hop around the room, collecting a doughnut for each person in the circle. As kids each get a doughnut, they must hold it in their mouth while the group hops around collecting other doughnuts.

Once each person is holding a doughnut in his or her mouth, kids may sit down, untie their shoes and eat their doughnuts.

TURKEY TAG

The object of Turkey Tag is for designated pilgrims to catch turkeys (the rest of the group) by tagging them. Any size group can play Turkey Tag in almost any room (as long as everyone has enough space to move).

Begin by establishing boundaries. Then, if your group has fewer than six kids, choose one pilgrim. If it has more than six, pick more.

Explain that two types of creatures are in the room—pilgrims and turkeys. The pilgrims hunt for turkeys to eat at their Thanksgiving feast. And the turkeys try to escape. Whenever a pilgrim tags (touches) a turkey, the turkey must stand in one place, stick out his or her arms like wings, flap them and say "gobble, gobble" until the game ends or another turkey frees him or her.

An untagged turkey can free tagged turkeys by tapping them on the head. But after a turkey's been caught three times, he or she becomes a pilgrim and joins the hunt for other turkeys.

The game ends when everyone is either a caught-and-gobbling turkey or a pilgrim.

TWO TRUTHS AND A LIE

In this game, kids try to fool their friends. You'll need tape or pins, and for each person you'll need a 3×5 card and a marker. Give each kid a 3×5 card and a marker. Say: **Write your name at the top of your card. Then write two true bits of information about yourself and one sneaky, convincing lie. Tape or pin the card to your shirt.**

Ask kids to mingle. Say: **Your goal is to figure out which piece of information on each person's name tag is a lie. Each time you're fooled, you must initial that person's name tag. At the end of five minutes, the person with the most initials on his or her name tag wins.**

WATER-BALLOON JUGGLING

Here's a good way to cool off on a hot day. You'll need lots of water balloons for this game.

Have kids form a circle outdoors. Toss a water balloon to someone in the circle, and have kids begin tossing it around the circle. One at a time, add water balloons until kids are "juggling" as many as possible. Remind kids to keep the balloons moving.

Whenever a balloon is dropped, kids holding other balloons must throw their balloons to the ground attempting to get as many people wet as possible. Remind kids not to throw the balloons directly at other people.

WILY WARM-UPS

Sometimes kids need to "warm up" before they begin an activity. Or perhaps your group members' attention is waning during a meeting. Use these ideas to lead everyone into action.

● Nose Song—Have kids find a partner and sing "Row, Row, Row Your Boat" in unison while they each hold their partner's nose.

● Backward Writing—Challenge kids each to write their name and address backward (so they would look correct when held up to a mirror).

● Cracker Mouth—Get ready for some laughs. Have kids each race to pick up a saltine cracker off a table with their mouth (no hands allowed), eat it and then whistle "Mary Had a Little Lamb."

● Spin 'n' Sing—Give these instructions: **Get together with two other people. The first person sings the first line of "The Star-Spangled Banner" and spins around three times. Then the second person sings the second line and spins around three times, and so on until the song is finished. Sing each line of the song as fast as you can.**

● Pat-a-Cake Relay—Form two teams to run a relay race. The first person in each line runs to a designated point, touches it, returns to the line and plays Pat-a-Cake with the next person in line. This process continues until one of the teams finishes and wins.

YOU MAKE THE GAME

Move over Milton Bradley. Make room for creative games designed by your youth group members.

Form teams of five to seven. Have teams each find 10 different items in and around your church, such as a Coke can, thread, hymnal or rock. Have teams each work in a separate area of the room to create a game that uses all their items. Give teams each paper and pencils. Each game must have written rules.

After 10 minutes, bring teams back together. Have teams each write their game name on a slip of paper and drop it in an available container, such as a trash can or bowl. One at a time, have teams each draw a game from the bowl, making sure they don't get their own game. Then have teams spend the next 20 minutes playing the games.

Afterward, have adult volunteers name the best game, craziest game, most practical game and best use of all materials. Reward each team with a loud cheer.

ZANY OLYMPICS

Athletic and not-so-athletic kids score big in these Zany Olympics. Have fun with these four crazy events.

● Miniature Golf—Lay out a course of three golf "holes" in the churchyard with obstacles such as bricks, boxes, trees and old tires between the tees and holes. Paper cups laid on their sides and nailed to the ground are the holes. Have kids use brooms or mop handles for putters, and Ping-Pong balls for golf balls. The person with the lowest number of strokes for three holes wins.

● Water shot put—Fill a one-gallon plastic milk container three-quarters full of water and tighten the lid. Have kids throw the container like a shot put. Allow each person two throws. Measure the distance of each throw with a tape measure. Combine the two distances each person throws the container. The person who throws it the farthest combined distance wins.

● Javelin throw—Tape three drinking straws together to make a "javelin." Give kids each two throws. Figure the combined distance each person throws the javelin in two throws. The person who throws the javelin the farthest combined distance wins.

● Standing Long Jump—Give kids each two tries to see how far they can jump from a standing position. Deduct kids' heights from the length of their jumps. The person who jumps the farthest combined distance wins.

For each event, award 5 points for first place, 4 for second, 3 for third, 2 for fourth and 1 for competing. Total the event scores at the end of the competition. Give kids with the three highest overall scores gold, silver and bronze "medals" made from painted paper plates and yarn.

DYNAMIC DIVERSIONS

BIRTHDAY FACE

Kids love to make a mess, and this game will satisfy their craving.

Form teams, and have a volunteer from each team serve as the team's "cake." Have the volunteer put on a plastic-trash-bag "poncho" and lie down on plastic.

Give each team a sack of the following: a tube of decorator icing, a plastic decorator tip and 12 tiny birthday candles.

On "go," have teams each open their sack and make a "birthday cake" on their volunteer's face. Walk around the room and pour sprinkles into kids' hands for extra cake decorations, and encourage teams to make wild and crazy cakes.

After a couple of minutes, have teams stop decorating. Judge the cakes by applause, and give the winning team Hostess Twinkies.

For a variation of this game, decorate the face of each person on his or her birthday. Take a photograph and display it on a bulletin board during the person's birthday month.

BUSIN' BUZZIN'

Copy the "Buzz Sheet" (on page 97) to use on bus trips with your kids. Form pairs, and have partners take turns answering the questions. For added fun, have kids switch partners for each section of the handout.

CALLING ALL CHEFS

If you want to have refreshments for your next holiday retreat or overnighter but no one volunteers to bring them, sponsor a contest. Have young people each bring their favorite homemade dessert. (Parents can help a little in making the dessert.) Tell teenagers they can't

BUZZ SHEET

Discuss the questions with your partner.

Getting Started

1. What is your favorite, and why?
   - place to go on a vacation
   - way to travel
   - place to spend the night
   - place to eat

Feeling Comfortable

2. When was the last time you felt one of these, and why?
   - happy
   - cool
   - zany
   - put down
   - religious
   - embarrassed

The Long Stretch

3. Which three menu items best describe your feelings now, and why?
   - hamburger
   - Cherry Coke
   - Oreo cookies
   - milkshake
   - pizza
   - Jell-O

The Home Stretch

4. Which best describes how you see God, and why?
   - a stranger
   - a friend
   - a relative
   - a police officer
   - an alien
   - a father or mother

tell anyone what dessert they made. At the get-together, have everyone taste the desserts and vote for the best-tasting one.

You'll have a great response and enough snacks for everyone.

CHRISTMAS-CAROL CONFUSION

Try this hilarious twist of musical fun at Christmas gatherings.

Gather songbooks that include religious and secular carols. Select the titles of several carols, write them on slips of paper and put the slips in a bowl.

Form trios. Have each trio draw two carols from the bowl. Give trios time to practice singing the words of one song to the tune of the other. It takes a little discipline, but the results are worth it when a trio sings "The First Noel" to the tune of "Jingle Bells"! Award a Christmas ornament, tape or other prize to the best performers.

CHURCH FAMILY FEUD

Here's an idea for drawing your congregation into your youth ministry.

Create a survey with 15 or 20 questions that could have multiple answers, such as "What is your favorite hymn?" or "What is your favorite table game?" Hand it out to church members before or after worship. Use the survey answers to organize your own Church Family Feud game show. Invite parents. Form two teams of kids and adults, pick an emcee and ask teams to decide the most popular answers to the survey questions.

COLLISION!

Crack up your kids with this simple activity that requires only a whistle and a few chairs.

Place all the chairs in a circle. Have kids each sit in a chair. Remove empty chairs from the circle. Explain that when you blow your whistle, kids should each change seats as fast as possible with someone on the *opposite* side of the circle.

To keep kids hopping, blow the whistle every three or four seconds.

After kids have bumped heads a few times, consider the following variations:

● Strobe Light—Play the same game but with a strobe light as the only light. Kids will lose their sense of direction and bump into each other.

● Light Switch—Instead of a whistle, flick the lights off to indicate time for kids to move. When the lights come back on, kids must freeze where they are. Turn lights on and off every three or four seconds to keep kids moving.

CREATIVE ANNOUNCEMENT RELAY

Use this creative relay to grab kids' attention.

Form as many teams of three to seven kids as you have announcements to make. Before the meeting, gather for each team a snack-pack-size box of Cheerios, a can of diet soft drink, a bag of shelled peanuts, a heavy blanket and a balloon. Write each announcement on a slip of paper, insert it in a balloon and blow up the balloon. Then tape the balloons to the floor in the front of the room.

Line up the teams in single file. Tell team members to alternate doing each step until someone on

their team pops a balloon. Each team will pop one of the balloons. Give each team a photocopy of the "Rollicking Relay" handout below.

The team that finishes first should read its announcement first, and so on.

ROLLICKING RELAY

#1—Eat a snack-pack-size box of Cheerios, and tag the next person.

#2—Chug a can of diet soft drink, and tag the next person.

#3—From at least 2 feet away, toss three shelled peanuts into the mouth of the next person.

#4—Tag the next person.

#5—Pull a blanket across the room with the next person in line sitting on it.

#6—Tag the next person.

#7—Dash to the front of the room and sit on one of the balloons taped to the floor. Find the message that was inside the balloon. Then stay up front.

CUSTOM SAND CASTLES

Here's a way to have fun on the beach, no matter where you live!

Form teams of two or three, and give each team a box full of sand, a pail of water and sculpting tools. Instruct each team to build a "designer" sand castle, made specifically for one of the following:

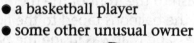

- a shark
- an Eskimo
- Tarzan
- a caterpillar
- an amusement park-owner
- a surfer
- a basketball player
- some other unusual owner

Allow teams 10 to 15 minutes to each complete their creation, then ask each team to lead the group on a guided tour of its castle. Unusual features and special additions should be explained. Award prizes for the most unique sand castles.

DINNER TO GO

This activity builds community while your kids walk, talk, eat and work together in teams. If necessary, adapt the directions on the "Dinner to Go!" sheet (page 104) to fit your area.

Form teams of three or more. Give teams each a single die, the "Dinner to Go!" directions and a grocery bag with three or more of each of the food items named. The amount of food items should correspond to the number of kids on each team. Set a time to return to church. Make sure each team has a watch.

DINNER TO GO!

Instructions: Go out the front door of the church and turn right. When you reach the corner, have one person roll your die. Everyone gets to eat one item from the grocery bag according to the following code.

If you roll a **1**: eat your sandwich

2: eat your fruit

3: eat your chips

4: eat your pickle

5: eat your cookie

6: guzzle your canned drink

If the number you roll is uneven, go straight ahead one block. If the number is even, turn right and go one block. Every time you reach a corner you must roll your die once. If you've already eaten the item corresponding to the number rolled, don't eat anything at that corner. Return to the church at _____ o'clock even if you haven't finished your meal.

DISABLED RELAY

Here's a fun activity that helps kids relate better to disabled people.

Tell group members they're going to run a relay of simple tasks but they'll have special instructions. Form teams of six. Give each team its envelope of beginning directions, containing six slips of paper copied and cut apart from the "Instructions" handout (page 106). Tell teams each team member must take one slip and obey its instructions. Also tell kids all team members must stay together during the relay. Distribute blindfolds to all team members who are now blind. Photocopy the following slips for each team, giving teams different stopping points.

At the first stopping points, each team finds pencils and paper, and a slip of paper that says:

Two members of your team can no longer walk and must be carried for the duration of the relay.

Your task at this stop: Everyone must write his or her name without using hands.

When you've all completed the task, go to

_____.

At the second stopping points, each team finds six crackers and a slip of paper that says:

One more member of your team can't walk and

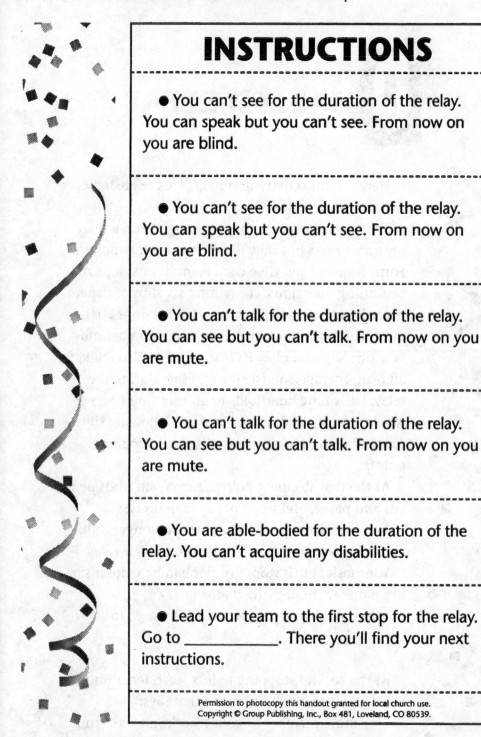

INSTRUCTIONS

● You can't see for the duration of the relay. You can speak but you can't see. From now on you are blind.

● You can't see for the duration of the relay. You can speak but you can't see. From now on you are blind.

● You can't talk for the duration of the relay. You can see but you can't talk. From now on you are mute.

● You can't talk for the duration of the relay. You can see but you can't talk. From now on you are mute.

● You are able-bodied for the duration of the relay. You can't acquire any disabilities.

● Lead your team to the first stop for the relay. Go to _____. There you'll find your next instructions.

must be carried for the duration of the relay. Another member is suddenly mute and can't talk for the duration of the relay.

Your task at this stop: Everyone must eat a cracker. When you've all completed the task, go to

_____.

The third stopping points should be near where the relay began.

At the third stopping points, each team finds a blindfold, six inflated balloons and a slip of paper that says:

One more member of your team is blind for the duration of the relay.

Your task at this stop: Everyone must pop a balloon.

When you've all completed the task, return to the place where you began this relay.

When you're done, discuss kids' actions and feelings.

EGG PLUNGE

Here's an "egg-zacting" challenge for your kids.

Have kids pair up and stand facing each other, about 6 feet apart. Give one partner in each pair a hard-boiled egg, and give the other partner a coffee mug full of water. Have partners with eggs each try to toss their egg into their partner's mug. If a pair's egg misses the cup, that pair is out of the competition. Have pairs continue tossing eggs—standing one step farther apart each round until one pair remains.

You may substitute rubber balls for hard-boiled eggs.

EGG PRESS

Kids will scramble in this game.

Form pairs. Call out body parts such as left shoulders, right hips and left ears. Have pairs each hold up a hard-boiled egg using their specified body parts and, without using their hands to keep the egg in place, compete in a 50-yard dash. Change body parts after each race.

Afterward, have kids eat the hard-boiled eggs (if they haven't dropped them too many times).

FRIENDLY FROLIC

Prior to the event, hide a "treasure" such as a bag of home-baked cookies somewhere on the church grounds. Ask kids each to bring a Frisbee and a picnic food to share. Have extra Frisbees on hand.

Have kids use their Frisbees as paper-plate holders for the picnic meal.

Then attach a different clue about the hidden treasure location to the bottom of each Frisbee. A sample clue might be "near a place of note," meaning near an organ or piano. Form two teams. Have kids on team 1 surround the kids on team 2. Give the Frisbees to team 1.

Tell kids the goal of the game is to find the hidden treasure. The only way to find the treasure is to gather clues taped to the Frisbees. And no one can read a clue until he or she has caught a Frisbee with a clue attached. Give kids on team 1 five seconds to throw their Frisbees to their team members standing across the circle from them. Have kids on team 2 try to intercept the Frisbees.

Then have teams each use their captured clues to find the treasure. Once the treasure is found, encourage the winning team to share it with the other team.

GREASED-PIG CHASE

Ask kids to wear old clothing. Form two teams, and have one person on each team be a "pig." Use string to tie plastic garbage bags over each pig's torso and legs. Spread salad oil on the plastic.

Mark out two circles 15 feet in diameter and put a "greased pig" in the middle of each one. The goal is for each team to carry outside of the circle the other team's greased pig. The team that moves the greased pig outside of the circle first wins.

HAVE-A-BAG-PARTY

Here's fun in a bag! Plan a party using these ideas:

● Play games using bags, such as a three-legged race in which partners each put one leg into a bag and run side by side.

● Form teams. Then for each team, wad up and stuff a complete newspaper inside a bag. The team that puts its newspaper back together first wins.

● Put various objects inside a bag, and have kids

make up a prayer of thanks to God based on the objects they pull out of the bag.

HOLY WATER CHARADES

Here's a fun idea for helping kids learn about the Bible while you're lounging at the local pool.

Play Charades using Bible stories that involve water; for example:

- Noah's ark (Genesis 6—8)
- Israelites crossing the Red Sea (Exodus 14:13-31)
- water coming from a rock for the Israelites (Exodus 17:1-7)
- Jonah and the whale (Jonah)
- the baptism of Jesus (Matthew 3:13-17)
- Jesus calling his disciples (Matthew 4:18-20)
- Jesus and the disciples in the storm-tossed boat (Matthew 8:23-27)
- Jesus preaching from a boat in the Sea of Galilee (Matthew 13:1-2)
- Jesus walking on the water (Matthew 14:22-33)
- Paul shipwrecked on Malta (Acts 27:14-44)

HOT POTATO CONVERSATION

Try this great game to get kids talking!

Form groups of four to six. Have groups each stand in a circle. Provide each group with a ball. Tell kids you're going to play Hot Potato Conversation. One person begins the game and the conversation by making a comment or asking a question. He or she bounces the ball to someone else, who must carry on the conversation by making a related statement or by asking a question. This second person then bounces the ball to a third person, who must also make a statement or ask a question that continues the conversation. If a player can't think of anything to say within five seconds, he or she is out. Play until there's a winner in each group.

JUMP-ROPE MANIA

Have kids work together to complete these jump-rope relays:

● Create the longest workable jump rope.

● Use the most unusual materials for a jump rope (such as shirts, socks, licorice, shoelaces or telephone cords).

● See how many kids can jump one rope at one time. See who can jump rope the longest.

When kids finish, ask them each to say one thing they learned about someone in the group.

A KISSY-PRINT CONTEST

This Valentine's Day activity sends everyone into giggles.

Before the contest, number white sheets of $8^{1}/_{2} \times 11$ paper, one for each person in your group. Have kids each put on lipstick—yes, even the guys. Then have each person secretly smack his or her "kissy-print" on a numbered sheet of paper. Tell kids not to let anyone see their kissy-print or the number on their paper. Make a list of which person's lip prints appear on which numbered paper.

Then tape the kissy-prints to the wall. Let kids judge the prints for kissability. Or they can guess which lip prints belong to who. Add your own judging categories—the possibilities are endless. And so are the giggles.

LOVIN' SPOONFULS

Kids will find a heaping spoonful of fun in this game.

Form two teams, and have each team form pairs. Give partners each a teaspoon. Place a baseball or tennis ball at the other end of the room. Have the

first set of partners in each line run to the ball, pick it up with their teaspoon and carry it back to the next pair in line. Have that pair take it from them, without letting the ball touch the floor or anybody's hands, run it to the other end of the room and then return to tag the next pair. Keep it up until one team wins.

Man THE LIFEBOATS!

Gather 12 heavy-duty paper plates and number them clearly, 1 through 12. Find an open area outside with plenty of room. Arrange the numbered plates, in order, into a square—leaving a large, center area "fenced in" by the plates. Secure the plates by pounding two nails through each plate into the ground. Have kids sit inside the square of plates.

Say: **You're passengers on a sinking ship. The plates surrounding you represent lifeboats. But some lifeboats need repair and will sink if used, so I'll let you know which lifeboats are safe to "board." Each lifeboat can hold only five people; and only the first five to place one foot on a correct plate will be safely "aboard." The first five kids to board a lifeboat will get 1,000 points each; those who are too late will receive no points**

for that round. I'll call out the numbers of the available lifeboats while you remain seated. Then when I blow the whistle, rush to one of the boats I've called out and "jump in." When I blow the whistle again, return to the center, sit down and wait for the next round to begin. Each of you is responsible to keep your own score through each round.

Provide one available lifeboat for every 10 kids. For example, if you have 10 or fewer kids, only one lifeboat is available. If you have 25 kids, call out three lifeboat numbers. Each round, vary the ones you choose. After five or six rounds, ask for each kid's point total and determine the high scorers. Award each winner a roll of Life Savers.

MOTHER'S DAY SCAVENGER HUNT

Liven up Mother's Day for your group members with a new scavenger hunt. Form teams, and assign an adult driver and a car to each team. Each team has one hour to round up the following five items and return to the church:

1. a gift your mother gave you before you reached kindergarten

2. your mother's purse

3. an item you wore as a baby

4. your mother's high school senior picture

5. your mother

Allow kids who don't live with their mothers to substitute items related to their fathers or guardians.

Say: **Each team member must collect at least one item, so for time's sake you'll need to determine who can collect which items the easiest. Your team must stay together the entire time. If you're not back at the church in one hour you'll be disqualified. The team that returns the fastest with all five items or with the most at the end of the hour wins.**

Give kids each a rose or other appropriate gift to give to their mom.

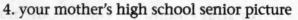ASS THE SHOE

Place all the chairs in a tight circle.

Explain that kids will pass a person's shoes around the circle. The trick is that kids may use only their feet to pass the shoes.

Ask for a volunteer or pick someone. Have this person slip off his or her right shoe and pass it with his or her feet to the right. That person must then pass it to the next person in the circle. Meanwhile, the left shoe should be passed to the left. Remind kids they may not kick the shoes around the circle or pick them up. They must slip each shoe over the toe of their own shoe to pass it along. If a shoe is dropped, it must be picked up by the person who dropped it using his or her feet only. Time how long it takes for the volunteer to receive the shoes back.

For fun, have multiple volunteers pass shoes at the same time. This gets interesting when shoes cross paths.

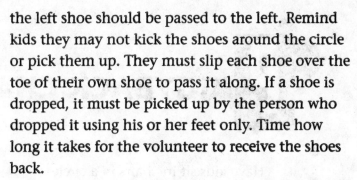

PEOPLE MACHINES

Form teams of four to eight. Whisper the name of a machine to each team. Tell the team members to use *every* person and make the machine with their bodies. Allow time for each team to decide how to make its machine and practice the movements.

Have all team members sit while you call one team at a time to demonstrate its machine. See if the other team can guess the machine. Applaud when each team is finished.

PIGGYBACK CHAIRS

Have kids sit in chairs in a circle.

Tell kids to quickly move to a new chair on your signal (a whistle or a yell). Move kids around a few times before continuing with the next portion of the game.

After kids have moved around a bit, give them this new rule: When they hear the signal, kids must each sit on a chair with another person (one person on the other's lap). Play this way for a while, telling kids they must have a new "partner" each time they change seats.

Keep things moving, and encourage kids to be seated quickly.

After playing this way for a few minutes, you can increase the number of people per chair to three, four or five. But be sure the chairs your kids are using won't break or fold under the weight of a large group.

This is a fast-paced activity which gets everyone involved quickly and does not require any special tools or a whole lot of space. And it's a fun way to form groups for discussion. After kids sit in piles of three or four a few times, have them stay with their last piggyback partners to form a discussion group.

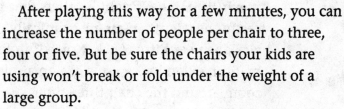

SCHOOL DAZE PROGRESSIVE RELAY

Try this fun relay about the "joys" of school.

Make a set of five 3×5 "School Daze" cards with the following information written on them:

Card #1—Shout the correct answers to:

- $2 \times 2 = ?$
- $4 \times 7 = ?$
- $6 \times 8 = ?$
- $6 \times 12 = ?$

Card #2—Together, shout the answers or do the activity required for each historic statement.

- In 1492, Columbus sailed the ocean blue and discovered _____.

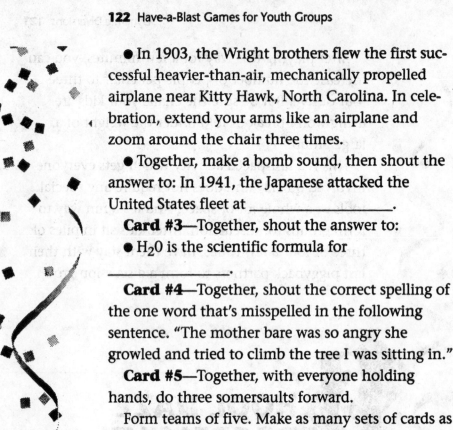

● In 1903, the Wright brothers flew the first successful heavier-than-air, mechanically propelled airplane near Kitty Hawk, North Carolina. In celebration, extend your arms like an airplane and zoom around the chair three times.

● Together, make a bomb sound, then shout the answer to: In 1941, the Japanese attacked the United States fleet at _____.

Card #3—Together, shout the answer to:

● H_2O is the scientific formula for

_____.

Card #4—Together, shout the correct spelling of the one word that's misspelled in the following sentence. "The mother bare was so angry she growled and tried to climb the tree I was sitting in."

Card #5—Together, with everyone holding hands, do three somersaults forward.

Form teams of five. Make as many sets of cards as there are teams. Line teams up single file. Set up a chair at the opposite end of the room for each team. Put a set of School Daze cards on each chair.

Then say: **In this relay, the first person on each team will run to the chair, pick up card 1, read it and do what it says. Then that person will run back to his or her team and grab the next person in line. Arm in arm, they'll run to the chair, pick up card 2 and do what it says together. Do the same thing with the remaining cards, picking up another teammate each time. The first team to go through all the cards and run back to the starting line wins.**

SHIFT INTO GEAR

Have kids sit in chairs in a circle. Ask for a volunteer. This person must stand in the middle of the circle, leaving his or her chair empty. Explain that the object of the game is for the volunteer to get to the empty chair before anyone else does.

Explain to the group that you're going to yell either "left" or "right" followed by a number. The group must listen closely for the number, then move the number of seats in the direction you called. Call out the next directions and number as soon as kids finish moving the appropriate number of seats. While all this is going on, the volunteer must try to find the empty chair and sit in it. Keep things moving so the volunteer and the kids in the circle have trouble keeping track of the empty chair.

When the volunteer sits in the empty seat, choose another person to stand in the circle. To help kids understand the game, start in slow motion and speed up as you go.

SLOPPY DARE

Ask kids to wear old clothes for this activity. Have kids volunteer to participate in these fun tests of determination and sloppiness. For each event, ask for volunteers first and then explain the event.

● Fill 'er Up!—Ask for three or more pairs. Give each pair a spray can of whipped cream. The goal is to use up the whipped cream by spraying it into one partner's mouth. The first team to empty its can wins.

● Shaved Santas—Ask for three or more pairs. Give each pair a can of shaving cream and a pair of

goggles. Have one partner wear the goggles. Have the other partner use the shaving cream to make the first partner look like Santa Claus. After a couple of minutes, stop the "decorating" and let the rest of the kids vote on the best Santa.

● Foam Peanut Stuff—Bring three oversize sweat shirts and three large bags of foam "peanuts" or newspapers to wad up. Ask for three teams of three. Have one team member on each team wear an over-size sweat shirt over his or her clothes. The goal is to stuff the most foam peanuts inside the sweat shirt while the person is wearing it. At the end of two minutes, stop the contest. Have the person on each team who's wearing the sweat shirt empty his or her foam peanuts. The team with the biggest pile wins.

● In Your Face—Make a pan of Jell-O, and cut it into squares. Set up a long table and bring plates, paper towels or napkins, and blindfolds. Ask for three or more volunteers. Place a plate with a Jell-O square on it in front of each volunteer, blindfold the volunteers and tell them to keep their hands behind their backs. The goal is to eat the Jell-O without using their hands. The first one to finish wins.

● Hairy Legs—Form teams of no more than three, with at least one girl on each team. Give teams each a supply of clear corn syrup and cut-up doll's hair or another substance that looks like hair such as small pieces of brown or black yarn, cut-up wigs or chocolate sprinkles. Tell teams they have three minutes to give a girl on their team the "hairiest legs" using the syrup and hair-like substance. Have kids vote on the girl with the hairiest legs after the three minutes are up.

NOWBALL GOLF

Take a swing at this new winter golf variation. With toy golf clubs, and snowballs for golf balls, sponsor a snowball golf tournament on church grounds. Designate boundaries and holes on your course. Have kids keep track of their strokes on a score card.

POON POWER

Give each group member a teaspoon, and have the entire group work together to move objects about 20 feet across the room. All spoons must be in contact with the object while it moves from one spot to the other. If an object touches the floor while in transit, the group must start over. The objects should be large, light objects such as volleyballs and pillows.

After the game, have kids talk about the importance of teamwork.

TAG-TEAM SUMO

Form two teams and designate captains. Prepare the room by marking off a six-foot square with strips of masking tape. Say: **This is an anti-Tug-of-War game which works something like Japanese sumo wrestling. Contestants will stand facing each other with legs apart, hands on one another's shoulders and heads down. When I blow the whistle they'll start to push. The first player to put a foot outside the square loses, and must tag someone else on his or her team to jump into the square and continue the contest.**

Have one person from each team step into the square to begin the game.

What kids don't realize is that strong, hefty players will eventually be worn down if they have to face several opponents, and may end up being defeated by an opponent half their size. Mismatches and upsets will create hilarious surprises.

This is a good game to use in conjunction with a study of "wrestling" against spiritual powers based on Ephesians 6:10-18.

UPLIFTING SCAVENGER HUNT

Instead of giving kids a list of specific items to seek out, give them this list of descriptions:
- something to cheer you up
- something to wake you up
- something to lift you up
- something to fill you up
- something to calm you down
- something to let you down
- something to wind you down
- something to slow you down

Have the scavenger hunt indoors or outdoors. Then have kids talk about the items they found and why they chose them.

WILD-GOOSE CHASE

Trying to help your kids find their way through the Bible more easily? Send them on a wild-goose chase!

Cut five to 10 geese out of thick paper and write a number on each. For each goose, write a corresponding "wild-goose number" at the top of a separate sheet of paper. Think of places in your church to hide the geese. Then look through a concordance and find the word and a scripture passage that correspond with the location.

For example: You decide to hide goose 1 under the altar. You look in your concordance and find the word "altar" appears in Genesis 8:20. On the paper titled "Goose 1" write "Genesis 8:20, word five." "Altar" is the fifth word in Genesis 8:20. Do this for each wild goose in your "flock." Have the last wild goose hidden in your youth room.

When kids arrive, form teams of three or more. Give each team a set of numbered papers of wild-goose clues and a Bible (the same version your concordance is based upon). Then set your wild-goose-chasers free. The team that comes back to the youth room with the most wild geese wins.

WILDLIFE PARTY

Make a name tag for each person. On the back of every two name tags, write the name of the same animal. When kids arrive, tell them each to look at the animal name on their name tag and keep it a secret from everyone else. At your signal, have kids each make a noise appropriate for the animal on their name tag—then find the one other person who's making the same animal noise. Ask each pair to sit facing each other.

Give each pair the following list of questions to ask each other and discuss.

● If you had the chance to be an animal for a day, which would you choose and why?

● Think about your family members; decide which animal each one is most like and why.

● Which animal do you think you are most like? Why?

● Read Matthew 26:47-50. Which animal best represents Judas? Why?

● Read John 6:66-69. Which animal best represents Peter? Why?

● Read John 8:1-11. Which animal best represents Jesus? Why?

Gather together and ask kids to give their answers. Then have an animal meal with hot dogs, animal crackers and brown cows (root beer floats).

WORLD'S GREATEST INVENTION

Here's an inventive way to beef up kids' creativity.

A week ahead of time, invite kids to bring their best ideas to a World's Greatest Invention Party. Make it an all-day affair. Spend the week gathering as much "stuff" as possible, such as appliance boxes, used posterboard, hubcaps, bicycle parts, broken small appliances, rope, tape, aluminum foil, markers, paint, anything!

When kids arrive, have them form teams of no

more than four. Have each team draw plans for its invention on a sheet of newsprint. Tell kids their inventions don't have to be functional, just creative. Suggest things like time machines or space capsules.

After teams draw their plans, turn them loose to build their inventions. Give them plenty of time. And feed them well—inventing is hard work.

For added fun, videotape the progress of each invention. Or take photographs to be published in the local newspaper or youth group newsletter.

Award prizes for the most creative invention, the ugliest invention, the most useless invention and the biggest invention.